JAMESTOWN  ED

D0175086

THE CONTEMPORARY READER

VOLUME 1, NUMBER 4

NF

Level

1-2

DEMCO

 **Glencoe McGraw-Hill**

New York, New York   Columbus, Ohio   Chicago, Illinois   Peoria, Illinois   Woodland Hills, California

CONTENTS

*You know rock 'n' roll when you hear it.
But how did the many different
sounds we call rock get their start?*

THE ROOTS OF ROCK 'N' ROLL

1   The broad form of music called rock 'n' roll
can be compared to a tree. Its branches reach
up, out, and all around. The roots of rock are
deep and wide. They go back hundreds of
years. Slaves brought the music of Africa to
America from the 1600s to 1808. They sang
as they worked in the fields. They passed this
music to their children and grandchildren.

***Years after his death, Elvis Presley remains the
King of Rock 'n' Roll to many fans.***

Slave Songs

2 Some of the slave songs were very sad. People sang about their hard work and pain. Newer songs came from churches. People sang about God and death. Other songs came from the country dances. Some songs had words. Others were meant to be played on instruments.

3 American slaves became free when the Civil War ended in 1865. Some African-American music started to be called "country blues." Singers with guitars traveled around the South. They sang at farms, work camps, and small-town dance halls. They were paid whatever anyone would give them.

Country Blues

4 Country blues singers had a certain style. They could bend their voices to sing not right on a note but *between* notes. This "bent-pitch" singing came from the way slaves called to each other in the fields. Country blues also had common patterns. Many of the tunes sounded alike. Many of

Slaves kept alive their music and dance from Africa; this gave rise to blues, jazz, and rock.

the words were about hard work, lost love, and the pain of being poor. Leadbelly and Blind Lemon Jefferson were two early blues singers who became famous. They were among the first to make records.

5   Robert Johnson may be the country blues singer whose songs most affected later rock 'n' roll. He came from the Mississippi Delta. This is a 100-mile stretch of land in Mississippi known for its fertile soil. His music is called Delta blues. "The blues is a

Chuck Berry (top) and Little Richard (right) were favorites of rock 'n' roll fans during the mid-50s.

low-down, aching chill," he said. "If you ain't never had 'em, I hope you never will." Johnson traveled around with his guitar. He got into plenty of trouble along the way. In 1938, when he was only 27 years old, he was murdered. Rockers such as Eric Clapton and the Rolling Stones say their music is based on the blues, especially that of Robert Johnson.

Moving North

6   As African Americans moved to the cities of the North, they brought the blues with them. By the 1940s, Chicago was the center of city blues. Many blues singers made records there. The Chicago blues clubs were big hot spots. The rhythms of "boogie-woogie" and "shuffle" formed the basis of Chicago blues. Singer Muddy Waters played a key role in changing the Delta blues to the city blues we know today.

7   Black music from the churches also grew after World War II. Mahalia Jackson's gospel sound helped form the styles of other popular singers, including Ruth Brown, the Dominoes, and, later, Aretha Franklin.

8   Blues led to jazz, and almost all early jazz was played by African Americans. By the late 1940s, jazz performers began joining big bands to create the "bebop" style. Bebop style grew from the blues. There was usually a strong saxophone in a bebop band. The music had a heavy beat. It was louder and larger than the older kinds of blues. It was dance music.

The first big hit for white rock 'n' roll was Bill Haley's "Rock Around the Clock."

9   Country blues performers started using electronically amplified[1] guitars. They began using drums and even harmonicas. Black teens started "doo-wop" groups, singing in rich harmony.

BANNER OF YOUTH

10 All the black music of the 1940s was called rhythm & blues, or R&B. Big-city radio stations spread R&B to homes all over America. In 1951, a Cleveland radio disc

---

[1] amplified: made louder

jockey named Alan Freed first called this music "rock 'n' roll." By the mid-1950s, Little Richard, Joe Turner, Fats Domino, and Chuck Berry were famous black rock 'n' roll singers. Freed and other DJs played their music. Teenagers, both black and white, loved it. Rock 'n' roll became the music of young people because it was a little wild. The electric guitars and heavy beat made it hard to keep from dancing. Rock 'n' roll set kids apart from their parents.

But it wasn't until white singers picked up on rock 'n' roll that it really took off. The first big hit for white rock 'n' roll was Bill Haley's "Rock Around the Clock" in 1955. The biggest rock star ever was Elvis Presley. He started out as a country singer. A record company signed him because they wanted "a white man with a Negro sound." Presley, Jerry Lee Lewis, and other white rockers topped the record charts. Many of their

For fans who grew up in the late '60s and early '70s, the Beatles were rock 'n' roll.

songs were "covers." These were songs that blacks had already recorded. Whites sang them in a popular style that caught the ear of more people.

NEW DIRECTIONS

12 In the early 1960s, the Beatles and many other British groups gave rock 'n' roll a fresh new sound. From that time on, rock moved in many new directions. There was the folk-rock style first created by Bob Dylan. There was soul music and Detroit's Motown Sound, which featured the tight harmonies of groups such as the Temptations and the

Supremes. There was the California sound of the Beach Boys. There was the funk of James Brown. There was the acid rock of Jimi Hendrix, Jefferson Airplane, and the Grateful Dead. Then came jazz rock, punk rock, heavy metal, and disco. Still other forms of rock followed.

13   Every now and then someone will say, "Rock 'n' roll is dead." But the rhythm & blues roots just keep on spreading. Rock music takes new forms and new names, and old-time rock 'n' roll is still played on the radio. So chances are, in one way or another, rock will just keep on rolling. ♦

QUESTIONS

1. What is bent-pitch singing?

2. Which singer was most important in moving Delta blues to cities of the North?

3. What was the first big hit for white rock 'n' roll?

4. Who gave rock 'n' roll its name? When?

5. What were cover recordings?

What is gold, and why do people lust after it?

GOLD FEVER

1   Say the word *gold* and people's eyes light up like the metal itself. No other thing has more value. Nothing else measures a country's wealth. To the people of long ago, gold stood for the sun god. The lust for gold has started wars. People have gone to the far corners of the world looking for it. It has been used as money. People may still use gold as money almost anywhere in the world.

2   Gold is a heavy metal. In fact, for the space it takes up, it is twice as heavy as lead. Yet gold is very soft. It can bend into any shape. It may be pounded into gold leaf[1] as thin as a coat of paint. Gold is very shiny. It is one of only two metals that is not white or gray in pure form. The other is copper. Pure

---

[1] gold leaf: a very thin sheet of gold

The cover of the Klondike News *for April 1, 1898 boasts of the region's gold output for the year.*

gold should be 24 karats,[2] or 1,000 fine.[3] Gold conducts[4] electricity but not as well as silver or copper. And gold will not rust. Nothing can change gold except a very strong acid.

3   During the Middle Ages,[5] people called alchemists[6] [al'•kuh•mists] tried to make gold from other metals. It didn't work. But today tiny bits of pure gold can be made from other metals.

GOING FOR THE GOLD

4   Much of the world's story involves gold. Conquerors Alexander the Great and Julius Caesar took over other countries. Their reason? They wanted gold.

5   Explorers Ferdinand Magellan [Muh•jel'• un], Christopher Columbus, and others sailed

---

[2] karats: units of fineness for gold equal to ¼₄ part of pure gold in a blend with one or more other metals
[3] fine: the amount of pure metal in a substance expressed in parts per thousand
[4] conducts: carries
[5] Middle Ages: the period of European history from about A.D. 500 to about 1500
[6] alchemists: scientists of the Middles Ages who tried to change less valuable metals into gold, find a single cure for all diseases, and discover how to live forever

Christopher Columbus and his crew sight land. They hoped to find gold in the New World.

to new lands. A big reason? They went for gold. The people Columbus found in the West Indies were already using gold fishhooks!

6   Hundreds of years ago, Spain sent ships to Latin America. Why? The crews went to seize gold wherever they could find it. On their way home to Spain, their ships were raided by pirates who wanted gold, too. Some of the Spanish ships sank. People still look for them today. Why do they go to the trouble? There is a trail of gold across the ocean floor.

7   People rushed to California in 1849. What was the hurry? There was gold for the taking in the streams.

8   Gold is still very important today. It is used in world trade and industry. Jewelry and other fine things are often made of gold.

Gold in World Trade

9 Gold has served as money ever since the use of money began. The United States, though, stopped making gold coins in 1934. Countries keep gold on hand and make it into bars of pure gold called *bullion*. It is sealed away. The amount of gold a country holds shows the strength of that country's financial system. The United States keeps most of its gold at Fort Knox, Kentucky. More gold bars are kept in the Federal Reserve Bank of New York. Other countries keep gold there, too. When one country settles a debt with another, the gold is moved from one vault to another.

Gold in Industry

10 Dentists still use gold to fill teeth. Gold is used to coat spacecraft and astronauts'

Gold has value in every country's economy. These bars of pure gold are called bullion.

helmets. Electrical contacts and many fine machines contain gold. And some computer parts are also made with the metal.

GOLD FOR FINE THINGS

11 Jewelers make rings, necklaces, pins, and watchcases using gold. It is also made into vases and bowls. It is bonded onto fine china. Gold leaf is painted onto store windows and stamped onto book covers.

12 Some things are not gold all the way through. Jewelry may be gold plated to make the whole piece look like gold. "Gold-filled" means a heavy coat of gold was used, most

often 10-karat. Gold-filled objects must contain at least 5 percent gold.

DIGGING FOR GOLD

13 Look hard enough and you can find gold in almost any rock or soil. But because it would cost too much to get the gold out, such gold is not worth the trouble.

14 A better place to find gold is within cracks of rocks that were formed by volcanoes. Over millions of years, some gold washes out of those rocks. This gold lies at the bottom of rivers. These are called placer [plas'•er] deposits. Some placer deposits are also found deep under the ground. They got there over many, many years as the earth changed and moved. In South Africa, gold

During the California gold rush, miners set up placer mines (right) and panned for gold in streams (far right).

mines may be 12,000 feet deep. In South Dakota, people have found gold 6,000 feet below ground. Sometimes gold is found by following a placer deposit. At its beginning might be a vein of gold ore.

Dressing Gold

15 Gold may come from the very top of the earth's surface, or it may lie deep under it. But it still must be pulled out from whatever joins with it. Getting out the gold is called *dressing*. There are four ways to dress gold.

16   The first way uses gravity.[7] Remember, gold is heavy, so it will sink in water. You can do what the miners in the California gold rush did. Fill a pan with the gravel that contains gold. Add water and rock the pan from side to side. The light pieces wash away. The gold settles.

17   Mixing the gold ore with another metal also dresses the gold. Mercury is the metal most often used for this purpose. The gold sticks to the mercury. Then the mercury is squeezed out. Only the gold is left.

---

[7] gravity: the pull on bodies toward the center of Earth, the Moon, or other planet

18   The third way of dressing gold is to use cyanide.[8] Gold ore is ground up very fine. The cyanide breaks up the gold but nothing else. The gold then washes out of the ore. This is the most common method used today.

19   The fourth method floats the gold out. Here, too, the gold ore is ground up very fine. It is then mixed with chemicals and water. That pulls the gold out by itself.

20   There is one more good place to find gold. It is often mixed in with other metals. People can dress gold from silver, copper, or other metals.

PURE GOLD

21 After gold is dressed, it must be refined.[9] Refiners can treat gold with gas or acid to make it pure. But in the United States, the most common way to refine gold is through electrolysis [ee•lek•trahl'•ih•sis]. The gold ore is shot through with electricity. Slowly, the gold comes out. Refined this way, gold can be as high as 999.9 percent fine. That's

---

[8] cyanide: a poisonous white compound
[9] refined: brought to a pure state

This view inside the vaults at the U.S. Bullion Depository at Fort Knox shows some of the gold owned by the U. S. government.

about as pure as it can be. The refined gold is then made into bars or bricks weighing 28 pounds each.

GOLD TODAY

22 In the last 500 years, 80,000 tons of gold have been mined. That sounds like a lot. But that amount of gold would form a block just 50 feet on all sides. Experts believe that only about 32,000 tons of gold are left to mine.

23   Almost no one tries to find gold in streams anymore. That gold is long gone. Today only large mining companies look for gold. Half of the world's gold mines are in South Africa. The United States turns out about 2.5 million ounces of gold each year. Forty percent of that comes from South

Dakota's Homestake Mine. The Carlin mine in Nevada and a copper mine in Utah also turn out American gold. Still, the world uses twice as much gold than is found in the United States.

24   Most gold that has been taken from the earth still exists. People know its value, so they keep it in the family. Countries hold onto their precious gold or spend it in other countries. Wherever it goes, and in whatever form, most gold will probably be around long after we have turned to dust. ♦

QUESTIONS

1. How many karats should pure gold be?

2. Where does the United States keep most of its gold?

3. What are placer deposits?

4. How many ways are there to dress gold?

5. What way of refining gold is used most in the United States?

6. Where are one-half of the world's gold mines located?

What was it like for the first men who walked on the Moon?

1 Since the beginning of time, people have watched the Moon. Many have wondered what it would be like to go there. In 1969, two Americans found out.

2 The start of the space age is thought to be 1957. That year a Soviet rocket zoomed into space and around Earth. The rocket was only the size of a beach ball. Just 12 years later, a man walked on the Moon for the first time.

Apollo 11

3 That trip to the Moon was a space mission called Apollo 11. It was part of a larger program called Project Apollo. Before Apollo 11, 10 missions had gone close to the Moon. The Apollo 11 mission would use the Saturn V (five) rocket to launch the Apollo 11 spacecraft.

LANDING THE EAGLE

July 20, 1969:
Astronauts Armstrong
and Aldrin take their
first steps on the Moon.

Far left: The Space Shuttle blasts off in 1991. The success of Apollo 11 helped NASA build the space program.
Left: Mission control tracks the flight.

4   It took 300,000 people to build the Apollo 11 spacecraft and the Saturn V rocket. Saturn V was the biggest and most powerful machine ever made. It was as high as a 35-story building and as heavy as 25 jet planes. Five million separate parts were used to build the rocket. It burned 15 tons of fuel per second.

THE LAUNCH

5   On July 16, 1969, the Saturn V launched Apollo 11 at Cape Kennedy, Florida. Three astronauts were onboard. They were Neil Armstrong, 38; Edwin "Buzz" Aldrin, 39; and Michael Collins, 38.

Destination: the Moon!
Apollo 11 spacecraft takes
off on July 16, 1969.

6   The final countdown
began. As a voice called
"10 . . . 9 . . . 8 . . .,"
Saturn V's first stage[1]
burst into flames. On
"7 . . . 6 . . . 5 . . .," all
five engines started up to
full power. A cloud of
smoke and steam circled
the rocket. At "4 . . . 3 . .
. 2 . . . 1 . . .," the big
clamps let go of the huge
rocket. At "0," Saturn V
lifted Apollo 11 up and
away from the pad. It
was 9:32 A.M.

7   The spacecraft made
an arch high over the
ocean, leaving a trail of

---

[1] stage: one of two or more
   sections of a rocket that have
   their own fuel and engine

orange flame behind it. Then it passed out of sight into black space. For 2 hours and 44 minutes, Apollo 11 circled Earth one and one-half times. Then the second and third stages of the Saturn V rocket went off. This shot Apollo 11 out of Earth's orbit.[2] The spacecraft was aimed at the place where the Moon would be three days later.

THREE PARTS

8 Apollo 11 had three parts: the command module,[3] the service unit, and the lunar module. The command module held the spacecraft's control center. Here, the three astronauts lived and worked during the mission. The service module held the power gear and food. The lunar module was the part that would come off and land on the Moon.

9 The command module and service unit together were called Columbia. The lunar module was called Eagle. Together, Columbia and Eagle pushed on toward the Moon.

_____

[2] orbit: the path taken by one body circling another body

[3] module: any in a series of similar parts to be used together

Apollo 11's astronauts were (from left to right) Neil Armstrong, commander; Michael Collins, command module pilot; and Edwin Aldrin Jr., lunar module pilot.

KEEPING IN TOUCH

10 The Apollo 11 crew kept in close touch with Mission Control. But Apollo 11 had to start coming down from the back side of the Moon. While it circled behind the Moon, Apollo 11 lost touch with Mission Control for a short time. That made everyone nervous. The spacecraft slowed down so it could be pulled by the Moon's gravity.

11   Apollo 11 went into engine burn right on time. Everything happened as planned. Apollo 11 came back out from behind the Moon, letting the astronauts once again talk to Mission Control.

LANDING DAY

12 The next morning, the astronauts got an early wake-up call. It was July 20, 1969—landing day. Mission Control went over the plan with Armstrong, Aldrin, and Collins. After eating breakfast, Armstrong and Aldrin dressed in their landing clothes. The special suits would keep them cool on the hot side of the Moon.

13   Collins stayed behind in Columbia. Armstrong and Aldrin left Columbia. Holding onto rails, the two climbed over into Eagle. Collins pulled a switch that separated Eagle and Columbia into two spacecraft. At that point, Armstrong said the words that have since become legend: "The Eagle has wings."

14   Eagle's fuel would last only 11 minutes. In that time, Armstrong had to steer 50,000

feet down and land on the Moon. Dust clouds made it hard to see. Large rocks were everywhere. Armstrong moved the craft looking for a flat spot. Time was running out.

15   The people at Mission Control held their breath. Aside from the risks of landing, they feared the spacecraft might sink into the Moon's surface. With just 30 seconds of fuel left, Eagle touched down without sinking.

16   "The Eagle has landed," Armstrong said. He and Aldrin waited for the dust to settle. Then Armstrong stepped out of Eagle onto a ladder. He pulled a cord that started a TV camera. One-half billion people on Earth watched Armstrong's climb down the ladder. At the bottom of the screen were the words, "Live from the Moon."

The World Watches

17 "I'm at the foot of the ladder," Armstrong said. "The surface appears very, very fine grained as you get close to it."

18   Then Neil Armstrong stepped onto the Moon, 109 hours, 24 minutes, and 15 seconds after leaving Cape Kennedy. His

next words were the most famous. "That's one small step for man, one giant leap for mankind."

19   Nineteen minutes later, Aldrin stepped out. Both astronauts felt almost weightless as they hopped around. Their 500-pound backpacks felt lighter than 100 pounds. They put up an American flag and a sign that read "Here men from planet Earth first set foot on the Moon, July 1969 A.D. We came in peace for all mankind."

MORE WORK

20 There was a lot of work for Armstrong and Aldrin in the next two hours. They packed up 48 pounds of Moon rocks. By phone, they spoke to President Richard Nixon. They set up test equipment that would continue to give us information about the Moon. And they left items in memory of the astronauts who had died trying to reach the Moon.

21   Then, it was time for Armstrong and Aldrin to leave. They climbed into Eagle and lifted off. They were able to get back into the

The first men on the Moon, Edwin Aldrin Jr. and Neil Armstrong, left behind the U.S. flag.

Moon's orbit and then hook up with Columbia once again.

BACK ON EARTH

22 Apollo 11 splashed down in the ocean and the astronauts were towed to land. They were kept away from other people for a few days. They passed all checks for any germs they might have picked up on the Moon. The three astronauts were fine. Later, the

world watched as a New York City parade honored the three heroes.

23   From 1969 through 1972, five more American missions put people on the Moon. But no one has walked there since. And no one will ever look at the Moon in quite the same way. For now we know that people have stood on that ball in the night sky. And somehow, it no longer seems so far away. ♦

Questions

1. In what year did two men walk on the Moon?

2. What was their space mission called?

3. Who were the three astronauts?

4. What is the lunar module?

5. What are some things the astronauts left on the Moon?

AMERICA'S NATURAL WONDERS

Which of America's national parks has some of the oldest and tallest trees in the world?

1   When you think of national parks, most likely you think of mountains and lakes. But our national parks include other natural wonders. There are beaches, deserts, caves, and forests. North, south, east, and west—our national parks are located all over the continental United States. You can also find them in Alaska, Hawaii, and the Virgin Islands.

HISTORY

2   The U.S. national park system began in 1872. That's when Congress passed a law making Yellowstone our first national park. Others were soon added.

Half Dome is a popular sight for Yosemite visitors.

Yosemite [Yoh•seh'•mih•tee], Sequoia [Seh•kwoy'•ah], and Mount Rainier [Ruh•neer'] were some of the earliest.

3   The National Park Service was formed in 1916. Its job is not only to care for national parks. It is also in charge of hundreds of historic sites. These include the Statue of Liberty and Ellis Island, Independence Hall in Philadelphia, the Freedom Trail in Boston, and the Vietnam Veterans Memorial in Washington, D.C.

A Look at Some Parks

4   Here is a sampling of some scenic [see'•nik] national parks. Perhaps you'll make time to visit them some day.

5   *The Carlsbad Caverns National Park* in New Mexico is unique [yoo•neek']. Here, you can see some of the world's largest caves. One of them, called the Big Room, is 285 feet high. It has a floor space the size of 14 football fields! Park visitors walk through

Left: Flowers bloom at Medicine Lake in Glacier National Park.
Inset: Lights dramatize the strange formations in Carlsbad Caverns.

underground passages to reach the caves. The ceilings, floors, and walls are covered with icicle-like shapes. They are stalactites,[1] stalagmites,[2] and crystals. These spires have taken thousands of years to form. In some cases, stalactites and stalagmites are joined, forming huge columns and pillars. Some of the shapes have names, such as King's Palace and Totem Pole. Besides these incredible[3] formations, on summer nights, visitors can watch thousands of bats fly out of a part of the cavern called the Bat Cave.

6   *The Grand Canyon* in Arizona is one of the greatest natural wonders of the world. Over many centuries, the Colorado River wore down rock to create the canyon. It's about 1 mile deep, 18 miles wide, and 217 miles long. The kinds of land areas from top to bottom range from deserts to pine forests. Roads run along the North Rim and the South Rim, each with endless scenic views.

---

[1] stalactites: icicle-like sticks of lime that hang from the roof or sides of a cavern
[2] stalagmites: icicle-like sticks of lime built up on the floor of a cave
[3] incredible: too unusual to be believed

Visitors can enjoy these views at the Grand Canyon (left) and Mesa Verde Parks (right).

Visitors can take pictures of special sights by tour bus. Many just want to enjoy the changing colors of the rocks as the sun moves across the canyon. People who want to explore the park further can take a mule ride into the canyon. Others can see the canyon in a thrilling raft ride down the Colorado River.

7   ***Glacier National Park*** is located in northwest Montana, close to Canada's

Sequoia National Park is home to some of the world's largest—and oldest—trees.

border. The park has more than 200 lakes and 50 glaciers.[4] Glaciers result from changes in Earth over millions of years. Visitors can see them from their cars. Or they can let a park ranger take them for a closer look on foot or on horseback. One special highway in this park has been named Going-to-the-Sun Road. At almost every turn, visitors see snow-peaked mountains and shiny lakes and waterfalls. In the fall, bald eagles and golden eagles arrive to feed on salmon. Visitors can also enjoy hiking, cross-country skiing, swimming, boating, and fishing.

8   *Mesa Verde National Park* was once the home of Native American cliff dwellers. Carved into the tall canyons, these stone cliff palaces housed the Anasazi [On•uh•sah'•zee]. These Native Americans lived in the area from A.D. 550 to about 1300. Some of the dwellings have more than 50 rooms and are two or three stories high. Mesa Verde National Park is located in Colorado. But it

---

[4] glaciers: large, slow-moving bodies of ice in a valley or on a land surface

is close to Colorado's borders with New Mexico, Utah, and Arizona. In Spanish, *mesa* means "table" and *verde* means "green." Spanish explorers probably named this park for the flat look of its forest. Park visitors can camp and tour the cliff dwellings by car or tour bus.

9   ***Sequoia National Park*** is home to some of the world's oldest living trees. Some of the giant sequoias are more than 3,000 years old. Looking straight up from the foot of one of them is like looking up at a 25-story building. The park's most famous tree is the General Sherman, named for Civil War hero

In these familiar scenes from Yellowstone National Park, a herd of buffalo grazes in a meadow area (far left), while Old Faithful spouts off for an expectant crowd (left).

William T. Sherman. At 272 feet high, it measures 101 feet around the trunk. Another feature of this park is Mount Whitney. It's the highest mountain in the United States outside of Alaska. Visitors can go hiking and mountain climbing. They can also enjoy horseback riding, snowshoeing, and downhill and cross-country skiing.

10   **Yellowstone National Park** lies in Wyoming and borders Montana and Idaho. It's the oldest and one of the most popular of our national parks. Yellowstone is known mainly for its many geysers [gy'•zerz] and hot springs. The most famous geyser is Old Faithful. It shoots streams of hot water into

Mount Rainier National Park is home to many animals, including the black-tailed deer at right.

the air about every 70–80 minutes. These jets of water can reach a height of 150 feet! Yellowstone has beautiful lakes, rivers, and waterfalls, too. People also come to see bears, deer, bighorn sheep, antelope, and buffalo. Bears have been known to come right up to cars and beg for food. But park rangers ask that visitors just watch the bears from afar. Besides sightseeing, visitors can enjoy boating and fishing, nature programs, hiking, and bird-watching.

11   *Yosemite National Park* lies on the western slope of California's Sierra Nevadas.

Yosemite Valley is known for its deep, straight-walled canyon. Cliffs rise up to surround the canyon. One such cliff has been named El Capitan. Waterfalls plunge hundreds of feet. The water flows to a flat river valley that was carved by ancient glaciers. The area offers sweeping views of the mountains, meadows, and lakes. Visitors can hike into the backcountry and to the tops of many waterfalls. One trail leads to Glacier Point, which rises to 7,200 feet!

12 ***Great Smoky Mountains National Park*** is about one hour's drive from Knoxville, Tennessee, and from Asheville, North Carolina. It is within one day's drive of almost all the large cities of the East and Midwest. Except for a road that goes through them, the Smoky Mountains stand unbroken for about 70 miles. They are among Earth's oldest mountains and rise to

In Grand Canyon National Park, the Desert View Watchtower offers a memorable vista of the Painted Desert.

more than 6,000 feet. Hikers can follow about 900 miles of trails winding along clear streams and waterfalls. Plant life is lush and varied, with more kinds of trees than in all of Europe. The mountain valleys seem to be screened by a bluish or smokelike mist. This look has given the Smokies their name.

VISITING THE PARKS

13 The national parks are owned by the people—this means you. A trip to any of the parks is a great way to see the country. Most of the parks are open year-round, except in bad weather. Many charge a small entrance fee but offer discount rates to seniors.

14   You can drive to the parks or reach them by bus or train. There are usually hotels or motels nearby, and many of the parks have campgrounds. You can write to the National Park Service in Washington, D.C., for information on all the parks.

15   We're lucky that people who cared about the land worked to get laws passed that saved these areas for the public to enjoy. It's up to us to continue caring. We can do our part as visitors to the parks by not littering in them. We can also vote for programs that keep these natural wonders beautiful for future generations. ◆

QUESTIONS

1. When did the National Park Service begin?

2. What is special about the Carlsbad Caverns?

3. What river runs through the Grand Canyon?

4. Who used to live in Mesa Verde?

5. What is "Old Faithful"?

Two sisters are each over 100 years old. What can we learn from them about life?

We're Having Our Say

1 The Delany sisters share a two-family house in Mount Vernon, New York. They have lived there for 30 years. At 104, Sarah Delany is the elder. Dr. Elizabeth Delany is two years younger—102. They are the daughters of a former slave.

2 Sarah and Elizabeth Delany have written a book. It's no wonder that *Having Our Say: The Delany Sisters' First 100 Years* is a bestseller. The Delanys have plenty to say.

SPECIAL PARENTS

3 Their father was born a slave. Henry Beard Delany grew up on a Georgia plantation.[1] Even so, he learned to read and write. He went to Saint Augustine's School for Negroes in Raleigh, North Carolina. There he studied to become an Episcopal[2] [Eh•pis'•cuh•puhl] priest. Later, he became the first elected black Episcopal bishop in the United States.

4 Their mother was Nanny James Logan Delany. She met her husband at Saint

---

[1] plantation: a farming estate usually worked by resident labor

[2] Episcopal: relating to the Protestant Episcopal Church, made up of the U.S. Anglican community and headed by a bishop

The Delany family: seated in the middle are the Delany parents, with Elizabeth to the right and Sarah to the left.

Augustine's. Both parents worked at that school for most of their lives. They raised 10 children who all went on to finish college. Two of them became dentists. One became a doctor. Another became a lawyer and judge.

5   Getting an education wasn't easy for these children. Their parents didn't have much money. Sarah and Elizabeth worked as schoolteachers in the South. They used money they saved for more education.

NEW YORK

6 In 1916, Sarah moved to New York City to study teaching. When she finished school, she looked for a teaching job in the city

schools. Sarah was told she would be given a class. But before that, she would have to come in for an interview. Sarah knew that being black would count against her. So she skipped the interview. Instead, she just showed up the first day of class. She became the first black teacher of domestic science[3] in New York City.

7   Two years later, Elizabeth moved to New York. She wanted to become a dentist. But New York University did not allow women into dental school. Columbia University did, so that's where Elizabeth went. Out of 170 students, she was the only black woman. And she was the second black woman to get a dentist's license in New York State.

BEST FRIENDS

8 Elizabeth and Sarah never married. In their day, many working women chose to remain single. The sisters share the special closeness of best friends. When asked to talk about their lives, they willingly answer questions. As they speak, one sister finishes the other's thought.

---

[3] domestic science: training in home economics

9   In spite of their closeness, the two sisters are very different. They have been that way since childhood. The family called Sarah "Sweet Sadie." Elizabeth is outspoken. She remarks, "If Sadie is molasses, then I am vinegar. Sadie is sugar, and I'm the spice."

GUIDING LIGHTS

10 The Delany sisters have lots of praise for their parents. Elizabeth says, "Everyone thinks their parents were special, but I *know* ours were." She goes on, "Our father was wise, and he was very proud of his family. We were and still are a loving family, very close to each other."

11   Sarah adds that their parents gave them strong values. They also got a sense of pride and independence[4] [in•duh•pen'•dunse] from their parents. From this came the strength to achieve. The sisters knew they would have to try harder than anybody else. That was because of the way blacks and women were treated in those days.

---

[4] independence: freedom from outside control or support

Race and Money

12 Elizabeth has strong views about race. "We were taught you didn't look at color. It doesn't make any difference to me whether you're black or white. It's the way you act that I look at." Elizabeth believes that racism is ruining America.

13 She also thinks Americans put too much value on money. "As people get more money, they get tighter. Selfishness and greed—those are two of the main problems these days." Sarah feels strongly that too many people fail to take responsibility for themselves and their actions.

14 But both of the Delany sisters love their country. "America's a beautiful place, and it's mine as much as it is yours," remarks Elizabeth. "I wouldn't live anywhere else. This is my home."

Family Help

15 The sisters look frail. But their minds are tough. As Elizabeth says, "At my age, I can say what I want. When you get as old as we are, you have to struggle to hang on to your

Travel was part of the sisters' education. Seen here at St. Mark's in Venice, Italy, is their mother (center) with Sarah to her right.

freedom, your independence. We have a lot of family and friends keeping an eye on us, but we try not to be dependent on any one person."

16   Once a fire broke out in their basement. After Elizabeth got it under control, she called the fire department. The sisters were left without heat. A relative asked them over for the night, but they chose to stay home—with or without heat.

KEEPING WELL

17 They share their beliefs about what keeps them feeling fit. Sarah says, "Exercise is important." They stay away from fatty foods. They may eat as many as seven different vegetables a day. Their big meal is at noon.

18   Laughter and enjoyment are important too. Elizabeth says, "We laugh and cut up[5] so much that the children next door must wonder what do those two old women find to be so tickled about."

19   Sarah and Elizabeth think the values they were taught are good for everybody. "Be your own person, owing no one. Help others. Be proud of what you are. And struggle for the best and most education you can get." ◆

QUESTIONS

1. What is special about the Delany sisters?

2. Why was Sarah afraid of the interview for a teacher's job?

3. Why couldn't Elizabeth go to New York University?

4. What do both women think of their parents?

5. How do the sisters keep well?

---

[5] cut up: to joke

In our land of plenty, people go hungry.
How can we help change this?

1 Margaret-Rae Davis stopped in front of the door. She didn't like to ask for help. But she couldn't seem to make it on food stamps.

2 Friends had told her about the food pantry. It helped people through tough times. These people had been laid off work. Others, like Davis, were disabled.

FOOD
for All

Clients working as volunteers at the food pantry help box up groceries.

"There is no shame," they told her. But Davis said, "I thought it would be hard to say I needed food."

3   Davis lives in the small town of Conway, Massachusetts. The people there are proud. The food pantry helpers understand this.

No Hassles

4   The food pantry in Ashfield, Massachusetts, is run by church members and clients. They don't ask many questions. How do you become a client? You say what you need. Tell what town you live in. Say how many people

live in your house. And give your first name. There are no difficult forms and no hassles. Respect comes first.

5   The food pantry serves eight towns. Every other Monday, 25 to 30 people show up for food. Some are regulars. Others come only when in need. The food pantry feeds about 75 people from all eight towns. Davis first went to the pantry in 1992. She says, "I've never felt bad. They make everyone feel good about coming here."

High Quality

6   There's another good feature about the pantry. The quality of the food is high. The pantry gets fresh vegetables from a nearby farm, which raises crops only for the needy. The harvest goes to places all over the state. It goes to shelters, soup kitchens, pantries, and inner-city farm stands.

7   On Monday morning, two volunteers are at work in the Ashfield food pantry. They are also clients. Today there is a good supply. On the shelves are cereal, juice, soup, pasta, raisins, cheese, and more. There are also

The Ashfield food pantry takes pride in the quality of fresh produce it provides for its clients.

leeks, corn, peppers, and cabbage from the farm. They divide the food into boxes. Large families get more than smaller ones.

8   The clients line up outside. They each get a number before coming in to pick up their boxes. The pantry also offers specials. Today these include soup and french fries.

FROM FOOD BANK TO FOOD PANTRY

9   How does Ashfield get its food? A lot of food in the United States goes to waste. But people decided to change that. Now there are ways to get it to people who need it.

Corn is delivered right from the field to the food pantry. Half goes to the pantry's shareholders, and half goes to the needy.

10   Supermarkets donate dented canned goods and damaged boxes. Farmers invite people to come and pick over their fields. Individuals and groups collect food.

11   Food pantries started in the late 1960s. Second Harvest, a Chicago-based nonprofit organization, began in 1979. A network of 185 food banks around the country belongs to it.

Large Food Makers

12 Second Harvest deals with the biggest food makers. Every month, these big companies get rid of a lot of food. They may want to change the package. Perhaps a machine put a wrong label on a jar. Or maybe a new product isn't selling well.

13 Ashfield gets its goods from a nearby warehouse. It belongs to the Western Massachusetts Food Bank, part of the Second Harvest network. When it opened in 1981, the food bank served 4 food pantries. Today it serves 80 pantries, soup kitchens, and shelters. In 1993, these agencies[1] served about 120,000 people.

Growing Fresh Food

14 Most food banks deal with prepared, canned, and boxed food. The Western Massachusetts Food Bank wanted to offer fresh food, too. In 1989, they started to grow crops to make vegetarian chili. They grew tomatoes, carrots, onions, and peppers on one acre of borrowed land. The next year, they

---

[1] agencies: places or offices that do business for another

Workers at a food bank farm harvest potatoes.

borrowed even more land to grow more vegetables. By the third year, they had eight acres. They sold some of the crop to the public to help cover costs.

15   Today, the food bank owns a 60-acre farm. To cover costs, it sells shares in the harvest to the public. The shareholders get about half the crops. The other half goes to the needy.

16   Some crops are trucked to Boston. The Greater Boston Food Bank sets up farm stands in the inner city. Neighborhoods

there don't have good fresh vegetables in their stores. Now people can buy corn, tomatoes, and other vegetables fresh from the farm.

17   The Western Massachusetts Food Bank no longer has to depend on leftover produce from supermarkets. In buying land, the food bank has put down roots. Hunger will not go away, but neither will this farm.

A colorful crop, sunflowers are another part of the bountiful harvest from a food bank farm.

FRESH FOOD IDEAS

18 The Food Bank of Central New York liked the idea first begun in Massachusetts. This food bank now plants on 40 acres of land owned by the county. In return for the use of the land, 10 percent of the harvest will go to a prison. This food bank, too, will sell other shares in the harvest to the public. But the rest of the crops will go to the needy.

19 The Second Harvest Food Bank of Northwest Pennsylvania turns to farmers for donations. "The food is there, sitting in the fields," says Sister Karen Kosin, who runs the program. She uses volunteers to pick the crops. But she gets short notice when they

In addition to prepared foods, food bank clients add variety to their meals with cucumbers, squash, and other fresh produce.

are ready. It is hard to round up a crew and trucks at the last minute.

20   Growing Groceries is a program of the Community Harvest Food Bank in Fort Wayne, Indiana. They give away vegetable seeds and seedlings. People grow them in their yards or in community gardens. The

food bank teaches them how to garden. It also shows them how to cook fresh vegetables.

21   Nearly 30 million Americans go hungry. And 12 million of the hungry are children. Soup kitchens and food drives have been run by the government for many years. But food banks, pantries, and shelters pick up where the government leaves off. They show how people can fight hunger at the community level. ♦

QUESTIONS

1. Why didn't Margaret-Rae Davis want to ask for help from the food pantry?

2. How does the Ashfield food pantry get its food?

3. About how many Americans go hungry?

*Why are the Olympics important, and
what has kept them going for so many years?*

Let the
GAMES BEGIN

1 Nearly every country in the world takes part in the Olympic Games. Every four years, countries send their best athletes to the contests.

2 The history of the Olympics goes all the way back to ancient [ayn'•chunt] Greece. In a grove of trees in Olympia, athletes met every four years. No one knows exactly when the games started, but the first records date to 776 B.C.

Swimmer Mark Spitz shows off five of the seven gold medals he won in the 1972 Olympics.

Right: The Greeks dedicated the Olympic Games to Zeus, the most important Greek god.
Far right: The Olympics in ancient Greece included horse and chariot[1] races.

ANCIENT GREECE

3   Ancient Greece was made up of city-states. Each was much like a country. The city-states were always fighting, but all the people looked up to Zeus as their highest god. They came together at Olympia to honor Zeus. They also gathered to show the strength of their city-states. The ancient Greeks even based their calendar on the four years between games. This time period is still called the *Olympiad*.

4   Over the years, the Greeks built temples for Zeus at Olympia. People came from far

---

[1] chariot: an ancient horse-drawn, two-wheeled cart

and wide to see the games and the temples. The Olympics were always held in late summer. During the games, the city-states put aside their weapons and kept peace with each other. Only men and boys were allowed to watch and take part in the games.

5   Early on, the games lasted only two days. The only event was a 200-yard dash. Later, at their peak, the ancient games continued for five days.

FIVE-DAY EVENT

6 The first day of the games was set aside for Zeus. A 34-mile parade led into the stadium.

Jim Thorpe was a Native American athlete who won both the pentathlon and the decathlon in 1912.

Judges dressed in purple robes came first. Then came the athletes and their trainers. The horses and chariots with their riders followed. Once inside the stadium, everyone washed in a common fountain. Then the athletes took a vow to play fairly. The judges, in turn, vowed to judge fairly.

7   The second day began with the chariot and horse races. Then came the pentathlon[2] [pen•tath'•lahn]. This contest included the discus throw, long jump, upright wrestling, javelin[3] throw, and the *stade*, or sprint race, that covered one length of the track. The

---

[2] pentathlon: a contest in which each athlete competes in five different events

[3] javelin: a light spear that is thrown for distance in a track-and-field event

third day began with a parade to the Temple of Zeus. Then the boys' games were held.

8   On the fourth day were foot races: the long race, the stade race, and the double-stade race. Next came wrestling and boxing matches. In the last event, the men raced wearing their armor.

9   On the fifth day, an important dinner honored the winners. Each winning athlete handed the judges a palm branch. In return, the judges gave each winner a crown made of olive branches. The winners then marched around the grove to the music of a flute.

THE END OF AN ERA

10   The games were held for hundreds of years. Even after the Romans took over Greece in A.D. 146, they went on. But more and more problems arose

Jesse Owens will always be remembered for his track triumphs of 1936.

Wilma Rudolph proudly displays her Olympic winnings. She was the first U.S. woman to win three gold medals in track and field events.

between the Greeks and Romans. And the athletes wanted more for their work than an olive wreath. This led to cheating among the athletes. The last of the ancient games was held in A.D. 394.

11   Stadium seating was not made of stone. Viewers watched the games from huge, sloping banks of earth that enclosed the stadium. The earth changed and moved over the next 1,500 years, so the temples and stadium became covered with mud. But in 1875, some people began to dig out Olympia. They wanted to stir up interest in the Olympic Games once again.

MODERN OLYMPICS

12 Not until 1896 did the Olympics start again. Those first new games were held in Athens, Greece, and involved many countries. Close to 500 athletes from 13 nations took part in 47 events. The U.S. team had only 10 members. It took them two weeks to reach Athens by ship, and they barely made it on time. But these 10 athletes went on to win 12 first-, 6 second-, and 3 third-place awards.

13   Since then, the games have been held every four years. But during the war years of 1916, 1940, and 1944, the games were canceled. In the modern Olympics, a torch from Olympia opens the games. A ray from the sun is magnified to fire the torch. In a relay, one runner after another carries the still-burning torch to wherever the games are being held that year.

WOMEN JOIN IN

14 Women first took part in the Olympics in 1900, playing lawn tennis. In 1908, women competed in figure skating and archery.[4] In

---

[4] archery: the art or skill of shooting with bow and arrow

Jackie Joyner-Kersee added her special style and flash to track and field events in 1988.

1912, they also took part in swimming; in 1924, fencing; and in 1928, track and field.

15 Many events have been added over the years, and some have been dropped. Winter games began in 1924. In the 1990s, winter and summer games were no longer held within the same calendar year.

DARK SHADOWS

16 The Olympics were never meant to involve politics, but at times they did. In 1936, the games were held in Germany. Adolf Hitler, the German Nazi leader, said that Aryan[5] people were better than anyone else. That was the year that Jesse Owens, an African American, took four gold medals in track and field.

---

[5] Aryan: relating to an imagined master race of non-Semitic white people with northern European features

17   More political problems were yet to come. In 1972, in Munich [Myoo'•nik], Germany, 11 athletes from Israel were killed by terrorists. In 1976, 30 African countries chose to boycott[6] the Olympics in Montreal, Canada. They stayed out because a New Zealand rugby team had played in South Africa. In that country, blacks were then second-class citizens. And 60 countries, led by the United States, boycotted the 1980 Olympics in Moscow. They chose not to take part in the games because the Soviet Union had invaded Afghanistan [Af•ga'•nuh•stan].

18   Another problem had to do with payment for play. It was a rule that Olympic athletes were not supposed to be paid for playing any sport. In 1912, Jim Thorpe, a Native American, won both the pentathlon and the decathlon [dee•kath'•lahn], which totaled 10 events. Officials learned that Thorpe had once taken money for playing baseball. They took back his medals, but restored them in 1982, after Thorpe's death.

---

[6] boycott: to join others in refusing to deal with a person, organization, or country to show disapproval or to force better terms

Eric Heiden skated his way to five gold medals during the 1980 Olympics in Lake Placid, New York.

19   Since then, some countries have found ways to reward their Olympic athletes. In the 1990s, paid athletes were finally allowed to compete in the Olympics. In 1992, the U.S. basketball team included the best professional players in the world.

BRIGHT STARS

20   The Olympics have featured the best athletes of every kind. Ray C. Ewey of the United States won 12 gold medals in track and field in 1900, 1904, and 1908. Another American, Micki King, broke her arm while diving in the 1968 Olympics. She finished her last dive and came in fourth. Then, in 1972, King returned and took the gold medal in springboard diving.

21   Also in 1972, Mark Spitz of the United States won seven gold medals in swimming, three in team events. Nadia Comaneci of Romania was the first to score a perfect 10 in gymnastics, in 1976. Claiming five gold medals in the 1980 Olympics, Eric Heiden of the United States was the first to win gold medals in all speed skating events.

22   More than simply winning, Olympic competition shows the best meaning of "a sound mind in a sound body." But perhaps the noblest reason for competing in these contests is to keep building friendships and respect among the nations of the world. ♦

QUESTIONS

1. How often are the Olympic Games held?

2. In which country did the games start?

3. Why is 1896 an important year for the Olympics?

4. Why are the games important?

Visions
of the
Night

Is there meaning to our dreams? Or are our brains just working overtime?

1   You go to sleep at night. It's a quiet time. You sink into many hours of doing nothing. Your brain is not busy at all. Right? Wrong.

2   Sleep may be quiet. You may not be moving around. But your brain is really very busy, and you are part of the action. Each night, you may go through four, five, or maybe six sleep cycles.[1] A dream is part of each cycle. In one night you might fly over your home, go out with the perfect date, or fight off an army of monsters.

_____

[1] cycles: series of events that happen again and again

3   Everyone dreams. In fact, nearly all mammals[2] dream. You may or may not remember what you dreamed. Or perhaps you remember only the last dream before you wake up. That is common.

STAGES OF SLEEP

4   Each sleep cycle has four stages. Each cycle lasts about 90 minutes. As you fall asleep you enter stage one, or the alpha [al•fuh] state. That's the time you might think of your best ideas. Then you enter stage two, which is a light sleep. Next comes stage three, the quiet sleep. Stage four, the last stage, is the sound sleep, or deep sleep.

5   The cycle then moves backward through stages three, two, and one. This time, however, stage one is different. Though shut, your eyes begin to move back and forth very quickly. This is called *rapid eye movement*, or REM for short. You begin to dream during REM, and after 10 to 30 minutes, your dream ends. Again, you move

---

[2] mammals: warm-blooded animals that breathe air and nurse their young

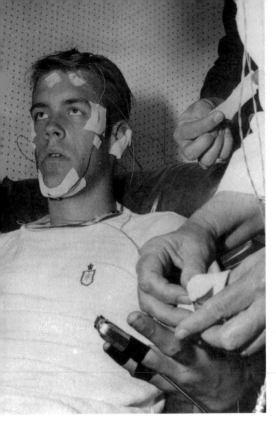

Randy Gardner is examined by a medical technologist while breaking the world record for hours of sleeplessness. Gardner stayed awake for more than 260 hours straight.

forward through stages two, three, and four. And so goes your night.

SEEING OUR DREAMS

6   You dream about 20 percent of your sleeping time. Your eyes move about as you dream. Does that mean you're "watching" your dream? Some tests done in sleep laboratories [lab'•uh•ruh•tor•eez], or labs, suggest this may be so. How can the experts tell? People

Light, color, sound, motion. . . What can you remember about your dreams? And what does it all mean?

who have been blind since birth have the same brain waves during sleep as the sighted. But blind people do not experience REM. They don't use their eyes while either awake or asleep.

TIME AND COLOR

7 You may have heard that dreams happen in a flash instead of in real time. Lab tests show that dreams don't run at high speed but in real time.

8   You may also have heard that not everyone's dreams appear in color. This isn't true. Everyone's dreams have color, but the

memory of color doesn't last. You may remember a dream but not its colors.

REMEMBERING DREAMS

9 If you have so many dreams, why don't you remember all of them? People usually remember only the dreams they have just before they awaken. Eight minutes into sleep, you move into the next sleep stage. Then it is too late to remember the dream you just had.

10 You are more likely to remember a dream you're having as an alarm wakes you. When you awaken on your own, your dream may already be too old to recall.

Sigmund Freud studied dreams and dream symbols to help people work out their emotional problems.

THE MEANING OF DREAMS

11 Most people wonder whether dreams mean anything. About 100 years ago, Sigmund Freud [Froyd], a well-known psychoanalyst[3] [sy•koh•a'•nul•ist] from Austria, studied the meaning of dreams. He believed that dreams are full of symbols [sim'•buls]. In other words, the parts of a dream stand for something else. Freud said a dream may be a way of wishing for something. People may

---

[3] psychoanalyst: a doctor who treats emotional disorders

dream about a trip they have never taken or a person they would like to know. He said that dreams can make up for things that are missing in a person's life. Freud also said that people block out feelings and wishes when they are awake. He believed that these thoughts, especially ones about sex and anger, are released in dreams. Freud helped people use dreams to work out problems.

12   Many books have been written about dreams and their meanings. Some authors match symbols with what they may stand for. But no list of symbols fits everyone. You're the best person to guess what, if anything, your dreams might mean.

SLEEP EXPERTS

13 Today, most experts believe that dreams tell about your wishes, your fears, and how you connect with other people. That's because most dreams have to do with very recent happenings. The brain explains the events of your day while you sleep.

14   Sleep experts also believe that you have some control over your dreams. Some say

Does your dream about Neptune symbolize your hidden desire for power, or did you just eat too much seafood for dinner?

you can even help yourself remember your dreams. They suggest that you tell yourself "I will remember my dreams" over and over before going to sleep. On waking up right after a dream, you can then write down the dream or record the story on tape.

15   Another way to control and understand dreams is to ask yourself questions. What do

you think your dream means? Does it have something to do with what's going on in your life? Did a real sound, such as the wind or a phone, work its way into your dream? Chances are, you can learn a lot if you give some thought to your dreams.

Time Well Spent

16 Can your dreams really tell the future? Probably not. You might dream about something that later comes true. Most often, there was no way to have known the outcome ahead of time. Whatever happens would have occurred whether you dreamed it or not.

17 We do know that dreams are important in our lives. Studies show that the REM, or dreaming stage, helps healthy brain growth in children. Dreams also help get rid of stress, build energy, and give balance to our lives. You might even say that dreaming is good for us. We can't help what we dream at night. And we shouldn't put more meaning into our dreams than is really there. But perhaps, if we take the time, our dreams can

Special laboratories help researchers understand what happens when we sleep.

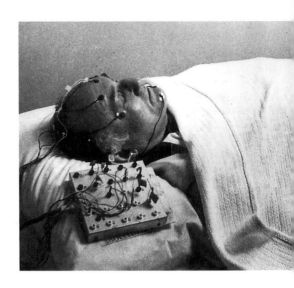

teach us something about ourselves. And we can use what we learn to help make our lifelong plans come true. ♦

QUESTIONS

1. How many stages of sleep are there?

2. What does *REM* stand for?

3. What do the experts say about dreaming in color?

4. Which dream will you most likely remember?

5. What did Sigmund Freud say about dreams?

GLOSSARY

THE ROOTS OF ROCK 'N' ROLL
Pages 4–13
amplified: made louder

GOLD FEVER
Pages 14–25
alchemists: scientists of the Middle Ages who tried to change less valuable metals into gold, find a single cure for all diseases, and discover how to live forever
conducts: carries
cyanide: a poisonous white compound
fine: the amount of pure metal in a substance expressed in parts per thousand
gold leaf: a very thin sheet of gold
gravity: the pull on bodies toward the center of Earth, the Moon, or other planet
karats: units of fineness for gold equal to 1/24 part of pure gold in a blend with one or more other metals
Middle Ages: the period of European history from about A.D. 500 to about 1500
refined: brought to a pure state

LANDING THE EAGLE
PAGES 26–37
module: any in a series of similar parts to be used together
orbit: the path taken by one body circling another body
stage: one of two or more sections of a rocket that have their own fuel and engine

AMERICA'S NATURAL WONDERS
Pages 38–51
glaciers: large, slow-moving bodies of ice in a valley or on a land surface
incredible: too unusual to be believed
stalactites: icicle-like sticks of lime that hang from the roof or sides of a cavern
stalagmites: icicle-like sticks of lime built up on the floor of a cave

WE'RE HAVING OUR SAY
Pages 52–59
cut up: to joke
domestic science: training in home economics
Episcopal: relating to the Protestant Episcopal Church, made up of the U.S. Anglican community and headed by a bishop
independence: freedom from outside control or support
plantation: a farming estate usually worked by resident labor

FOOD FOR ALL
Pages 60–71
agencies: places or offices that do business for another

LET THE GAMES BEGIN
Pages 72–83
archery: the art or skill of shooting with bow and arrow
Aryan: relating to an imagined master race of non-Semitic white people with northern European features
boycott: to join others in refusing to deal with a person, organization, or country to show disapproval or to force better terms
chariot: an ancient horse-drawn, two-wheeled cart
javelin: a light spear that is thrown for distance in a track-and-field event
pentathlon: a contest in which each athlete competes in five different events

VISIONS OF THE NIGHT
Pages 84–94
cycles: series of events that happen again and again
mammals: warm-blooded animals that breathe air and nurse their young
psychoanalyst: a doctor who treats emotional disorders

THE CONTEMPORARY READER
VOLUME 1, NUMBERS 1-6

The Contemporary Readers offer nonfiction stories—intriguing, inspiring, and thought provoking—that address current adult issues and interests through lively writing and colorful photography.